HOW TO MAKE WORDS OF RUBBLE

Isabel Sobral Campos

Cover art by Charlene Mosley and Payton O'Neal
Book design by Payton O'Neal
ISBN 978-1-7358365-0-8
Blue Figure Press
bluefigurepress.com

HOW TO MAKE WORDS OF RUBBLE

Isabel Sobral Campos

BLUE FIGURE PRESS

For Otília

Choral Ode:

A two-part improvisation or expansive moment of tragedy

Orchestra:

Distinct hum persists as textual backbone

Characters:

Trinity Altar: X (a subject); a daughter (Z); Grendel's mother, a resuscitated ghost

Grendel as corpse

Hurricane

Rock (and its alternate shadow, moss/grass)

Setting:

A wood

Time:

In the making of new horology

I.

An opera house of crickets
auditorium of stonebark
the chorus ~~a strike that line~~
predictable, exhausted anthill

Not an idyllic forest / / a conglomerate of trees looking on
THE SLIME OF TIME
Contrapuntal;
pellet-sprout
Contrapuntal;
semaphore-song

Irrepressible brainwater
I wear this dazzling hurricane (my ball gown
(I remove my plankton sandals to chew)...

The body that grows on my top body
& the body that grows on my bottom body

(A child in my belly,
A mother on my back
2-headed monster + me: (So Few Words I'd Like to Sing!

Trinity-Forest

Propeller-Scare

Mint-Apocalypse

X's Speech:

Look at the cloud's absorbable force—the vortex of indifference and lattice streams (slowly). A pressing insinuation overhead. Is it a button large enough for failure to observe? Your attention strays into the vicissitude of a schedule. Spelled words leave you nonetheless empty. I thought of this (as yet) unformed word (in which language I could not decide). Our dying, robust, & you who occupy an inch of earth often think of bones.

Rinsing my speech with bleach. Month-old soiled sheets. In these bits of hair, I exist. Blood, muscle, affect grind (my mood: small enough for a blur).

Thee blind ecology fills # rock. Thee filament hollow as gale tree
bursting with hurricane darts. Split tree is shaped
conch defangs undulating hemlock. Down below head on argillite.
Fragments impair her ability to think. All words for trembling
stumble beneath bedrock, arrayed in the draped forms of leaves
quaking through gusts, swirls.

Thee power enough to rattle thought
cowering blur
boundary cannot speak

I withhold words for storm in her native tongue.

Here a blank.   A roar.   Here an absence.

What moves the tulip?
If not spit, teeth?
The chorus sings:

Word for bone is OLIGARCH

When we look at the sun with shut eyes and see it is just another day. I respond to all troubling facts by seizing upon more trouble. Shedding my body's vines. Small gestures of time turn within me. Wrapped in slowness my motherhood weighs a child's golden weight. I comb her hair, flap her large ears, clutch the breathing slab in the palms of her hands.

Water tastes like westward, bleeds more sentient

Recognizing the aroma of day, curry of some anonymous neighbor, memory of summer as leaves trail to the ground

A daughter hesitates between spellings of the same sound:

> A left (maimed way)
> A warped manner

We move to the swamps lugging Grendel's mother upon our backs
Her gentrifying corpse
The sun juts open within a cloud that takes on a morbid shape

A daughter's first fears:

> Clouds shaped like monsters
> Mother monstrous
> Warlike motherpaws

Chorus relents X turns to Z a tilting melt on her cheek: she was
struck with a vision of
DERRIDIAN SLIME:
Word
Onto
Word
Onto
Word

Cooing daughter's universal speech
Her word for goggle is tttt for wind or widow water on raft for worm
as tree for glitter in spark sun Tucson
g word for Gotham

Is her total word a unanimous storm? I await in personhood
the calm of an ever-
embracing sound
a collective unctuous miming of lips
hurricane shriek dash tree trunk to sodden shrub

Z's speech cazooooliinnnn ....
                    zinzinnnncazoooliinnnn....

My half-rotten fingers swollen as top body grows detrimental to bottom
A black of word clacks stunningly present

                    Extant aching on tattooed filter of consciousness

Your raspy chant of spring fallow throat
In that a swamp exhales Grendel, spits him out

Thee word for storm is meek
Thee chorus' raspy voice grunts
in bottomless woe
Thee word thrashed upon spectacular wind
unbloodied outward sponging eyesight
flushed decisively
as universal cooing

Clothed in a staged snore and a tiny garb of light. I slump under
weight of wheatgrass calling on daughter
to wend back, the minute fire
with which I heat my feet, keep body
uneconomical sustenance. Every morning I count her breaths

In my voice the chorus swells with words clipped
to blur her between worlds
staple her to bark

Thee gale will pass her
Thee gale will not set her free

What is contrapuntal in this finality
(humid drip of changeless season?)

I collect specks of dilapidated house
the ancestral sentries
dirt, flint

On the stonebark stage with beehive humming in the wind pleats
I love you through the mist donning unnamed vestment:
inconsonant confabulation

The blinding darkness of forest conceals millenary accumulation of mother. We remove our skin from the future, (our lily ooze), to hang within the treetop grove. We build proverbial dark cave, becoming cavernous, bright black and gleaming. While winds shatter limestone in watery gusts. While we bright black withstand, wait (a turn, an endurance) while Grendel's mother's corpse bloats in its borrowed skin.

Scribe of hurricane
crustaceous cradle
of scripted tide

is levitant who calls on forest

Folded legs hovering   gruntlike

I recognize my eyesight as borrowed scent bestowed by the animal hormone that seizes me. When daughter asks with Z's collation, "what collage is this color from?" "what piece of wood goes here?" "what space is this I do not understand?" It is always a new uninvented iteration of swamp from the nether not of decreative force.

You who are sunflesh
not fog

Someone flits a plastic straw to the edge filming the controversy of human plot. Daughter unstitches each pronoun I have worn, each butterfly persimmon on the slaying ear attentive to the numinous between apartment building walls,

the shaking grace of storm, fist augury

honeycombed
consciousness

I bite tree

Predictability becomes unreadable
scribble on daughter's illicit page

Sapient stage, windswept
daughter and I linger like folded shades (doubling on second
darkness) and listen

OUR EARS FELT LIKE

The low lulling of being in the white noise between leaves
Even now, spectral doors haunt the forest
Grendel's mother whispers "we are inside an all-encompassing
womb whooshing with gunmetal sounds."
A reedy rock whistles. At another level, the womb's microbial silence

An ever so dim quiescent gurgle
An ever so slow bob
In shattered second

Grendel's mother distilled particle knows
        the bleeding udder of phlegm
             waking to daughter's insistent slippage of rrrrrr
               her regurgitated vowel/ / lungful cacophony

thee sounded plant threads through her body (fizz)
cosmic static gulping its way internally

FREQUENCY
in sonic periphery

Storm exists as prophylactic test tube
“I remained outside ligatures of terrestrial deafness.”

SO, CHORUS PRODUCES ELEGY

& THE ELEGY:

~~zapping~~

~~TRILL~~
~~TRILL~~
~~TRILL~~

~~zapping~~

~~(y) TRILL~~
~~(y) TRILL~~
~~TRILL~~

“Supersonic storm”
“My ear feels like a damp voice”
“My ear inside your voice”
“Slips into puddle”

=

The vesture of sound

“What does my ear feel like?”
“What does it feel like inside my voice?”
“What trouble to keep my voice?”
“What trouble to slumber in my voice?”
“What does it take to scrub a voice”
“Then dry it?”

A storm, not a sequence of answers

The nether not   rip & ripple
        battered wing
                    at which obscurity sprouts in atomic quiet
                        shuffle rustling
                      Grendel's mother scratching grain of voice

Each day the wrath of stunted speech, a failure to name something veridical about the atmosphere. Clothes become baggy enterprises of older selves & daughter studies my inability to order the passing. Optimal epiphenomenon of juncture when I sponge her tangled hair, we descend upon glug within unconscious ear.

Stillness bleeps against human edge.

Thee soothing guzzles belly
Thee gale making us caves

Grendel's mother drags words from my mouth, "The solar movements for which our witnessing remains still meagre"

The subject is terminal silence
The memory a place releases is how to make words of rubble

How (how much of silence can we (mesmerize))
The silence of a projected mind (interim dismissive of limit

What is the rub of silence, its gesture, its greed?
Can I see the color of silence in folds of noiseless?

Repetition is not death
Repetition is not silence
Silence's cape vaporizes thought
The subject is colonial
Heavy absence ahead of thunder
(blotted)
First Regression of Economics

At first, she lay awake without sleeping
I could place my phone facing down on my desk
I could say someone's name
What did you say? What did you talk about? What was it like to you? Had a very similar problem. Thought very similarly to you. What did you feel about it?

As many things as you can remember about...
As many things as you can remember about... about...about...about...
about...about...about...about what was said in depth, en masse, in passing

What you do to listen better what you do to listen more what you do to listen more intently more closely, more precisely, more imaginatively, more admirably, more stably, more more more more more more more
about, about the inact IN_ACT,

Chants the chorus:

I remember a sentence called child
It gazed at me
I gave it a name like O
The sentence gorged on air
like a very taut string
Full of tragic data, tragic results
Offering this liquid sentence to my child
Without explaining the ins and outs
Without confirming the exit
She walked in circles in search of a place to relieve herself
But couldn't find it
As if by refusing the very sentence that makes cities happen
That erects roofs & roads
I wiped the sentence clean, it made a mirror
For people with petrified sentences (like me)
That rippled out of hanging bellies
I decapitated a sentence that threatened me
Then rolled with its severed skull
The head stealing my sentient eyes
And gave a child with an O name
A sentence resistant name
Which may account for her reluctance to speak

Thee blind specimen droning diorite
Thee blind accoutrement

Deciduous flowing worm to which daughter's attention swerves. A traceable understanding undeniably causing the putter of sound itself to emerge. Softly as repressed volcano. Both daughter and I and my third body lift our chins up to the sky so that sound may touch us.

The soft frequency of our muted buzz in the interspaced interval of a sick machine. Surveying what has been hardwired, what unmoored. The gentle supine network of line folded on to line that spells daughter's fate onto mine own flesh. A microscope to observe the motions of sound, study of sluggish rebellion. While Grendel's mother renounces sight. When she speaks, "The gulag subsists in air:"

> Rhythmic muffling of myna bird on branch
> As woodpecker, street sweeper
> Passing squee, scrunch on surface of plastic

Temperature of hoot, sound of hot lava encrusted in diluted
consciousness daughter knows

I am consumed,
translated

Z's SPEECH:

As musician without direction inclination of lilting storm in repetition
Wave ! Wave !
There is a space between words when sound emerges
Bathes the screen with shimmering
pitch of brightness
Continuous magnitude
Where I speech into boiling as hot as cold as with them being permissive
WHAT with all the TIME in the world to LEARN
I study molecular movement of noise on small brain of small human
Motion suspended, blast do not show, refuses totality
In the gurrr And whyyysssss
I am din, daughter, observer of third body

Look
At
The
Sound

In time. There will be no time. My haunches crushed by Grendel's
mother clawing between these opposites.
Maximum effort to join the silent hum of grass.
On tenterhooks of connectivity awake to fleeing murmur.
Present on alien leaf, a gut.

Thee ornamental geld
lies prone & sleeping

~~JUDGING.~~ (torrential chorus sings)

The opera shapes an ending
  Voice induces hypnosis
But I do not press my palms to the child's ear
  Armed with Grendel's mother
Time wrapped in sundry weeds

Rapture of what in the brim (or boundary of thee), as daughter begins speaking a tongue in the notch of words I first modeled (resisting the ye, forcefully) while I assert my will, knowing it selfish, retracting simultaneously into tininess

Thee third body brands night
tectonically hissed in the angled ear
its treelined heaviness upon plangent inaudible
pitch of Grendel's wakefulness
I huddle small like a human
I scissor her wings from my back
my grey skin moans her leaving
We both see that rain is the color of ice, we see
the same mechanism of flow
melodic hollowness as love for daughter, as grasp MOST loved body
in trinity altar
ear follows tuneless climb of incense smoke
and (ye) whose piebald fur anthropogenic
storm raging against natural stage
study of pigment on windowpane

Thee tor quaking
Bedrock's aphasia gleaming

WHILE MY CRYPTIC EAR FELT SHADE.

I was freshly devised animal and my threefold existence disappeared
/ / along with incarnation-daughter / / I chased the incarnate ghost

A flicker of flood

If I described the telepathic trance whose soundwaves sculpt water,

erect and subsume waves to muscovite, of Grendel's mother,
daughter and I

riddled as supersonic mute entity, for water is dimmed contemplation

fibrillate the air, conclude our lesions
this openness greeting us
jettisoned grief of one thousand archetypal mothers

because churned clause claims that:

"The byproduct has reached point of saturation"
"The womb is ready for extraction"
"And syndrome of overridden futurity gradually incurable"
WHILE MY EAR BALLOONS.
(being silent cog awaiting maturation)

What is not revolver

But stalked
Filtering speed in acquiescence to knowledge,
What does the CHILD know in LIEU of MOTHER<
Not even Grendel,
can. say. that.

daughter's eyes, (theoretical zones),
woks
of uncertainty
:

Grendel's mother's birth is this horology we recognize as time
A diphthong on mist

I have seen eternally with borrowed corpse
And seldom to my exhalation
                              producing vocalise with chest frame
                                 averting thoughts from suicidal SLUR

                                 (You will dream in borrowed language
                                 (Assigned a totem animal to your total being

"The cannibalistic nature of labor-power is not unlike the yawning potency of storm," Grendel's mother says. There is irony in this. I grow tired. The stillborn dusk.

                                                            MY EAR
                                                            A-BENDING
                                                            WITH LIGHT

SCRAP FOR NEW HOROLOGY

FIRST

Nights ache. Windowpanes shatter.

The slow appoggiatura falters. Grendel's mother paces
in her fabricated time signature halting between glooms
Shadows timestamp my face
                                                            Night is neurosis, plummeting
                                                            irrotational earth, maternal

SECOND

The tempest whose transmarine tinge will erase the globe
                                                                        is here
                              halfway in tsunamic hourglass
showering antemosaic monument
                                                                  trigonometry applied

AGAIN

The sun extends midway between buildings. Daughter sleeps esoteric devolution I shatter with bloody hands. Grendel's mother won't leave until I breed a protective force. I have reached her diuretic vision of the world.

ZERO

Chronometry stabbed on rock.

SCRAP FOR NEW HOROLOGY

MULTIPLY

I expected it to move smoothly over liquid whose names are many.
To absorb spatial recognition (how do oceans and rivulets breathe
comparatively?), when daughter asks:

"How much in this estuary of glitter?"
How many mythic beings lift their hands before she shakes her head?
"How much air inside water?"

The delta she loves more than sky
(she waits at the cusp of water without looking back where I stand
rake in hand)

PARTITION

The age of tree in its distended chronology measures ear, diffracts,
jitters. Grendel's mother tells time thru the saline content of her belly.

I tell time thru weeds
Daughter knows it like bone

MOOR

Chronometry unleashed / / Wind curls uncloaking time

SCRAP FOR NEW HOROLOGY

is rubble

SCRAP FOR NEW HOROLOGY

Disordered clumps expressing condition of sediment
Variety of fragment epipleural on human

So many pieces with faces (granite lips)

Grendel's mother whose moves of stone sentience
Command me
Toward metrical footfall
plip
plip
plop

Gneiss speck in my throat
Snapping words with fragments
On years of daughter I chant beginning
My rock protectorate
Overlay
You brush the wind from my face with your small hand
Used to bathe an old mother's body
When Grendel as grief returns
Jutting through brickwork
Layered with scars
I have marked the stink of emotion
Each tree delineates past tremor
The rub of Grendel on winter's back

SCRAP FOR NEW HOROLOGY

PENITENTIARY

Fence, wall bears mark of flowers
or creeping vines through which my feet falter
is and is not an emblem of human inability to redeem
villainy of marked walls or fences with withered
unseasonal flowers for I who names and unnames
flabbergast at the ghost lurking in a name
surmises what flower in fence or wall must conceal
as door to and from the inescapable autocrat
fuchsia on fenced wall upon flaws of light
letterings of walled flowers
penitently deep

RUIN

inside of which my heart beats
    in the sluggish tempo
        of molecular meteorite

SCRAP FOR NEW HOROLOGY

PENITENTIARY

"It's getting late." Grendel's mother exhales winter.
Clouds spit drizzle.

Our threefold body gendered altar pops
strange soda / / tiny pattering tongues

Everyone gazes when sand bursts from the colossal hourglass
Turbine wind over crushed grass

Blackstone poses
Atemporal
The moth-choked world

RUIN(ED)

I walked drenched in my naked thought slumbering motherwise
Outside (time bowed surfaces)
Gravely walked in the center (of her spiritual name
(a glowing roundness spoke:

O STRIP MY BODY PARTS
OF ROCK FRAGMENT
O LINE THEM WITH MOSS

SCRAP FOR NEW HOROLOGY

TIMELY SOB

I wear taboo on my body as often as Grendel's mother speaks "from her dungeons" with her slow gesture of time (more than a mood or a substance)

Her constitution is craterlike
An abstract similar to stump in her moorland

NINE MOUTHS

Only motherhood withstands the cave a rock abhors
(Shut human eyes)

Each month sewed on skin

When it terrifies, it terrifies
Roaring (razorskin sheep)

An empty bowl that waits / / Sad fly with seltzer wings / / That burn fantastically / / Human dimension of emptiness / / Collecting the inner / / Floret juggernaut / / Scarred in stillness of singed quill / / Collecting the screeched elsewhere / / I will not know the so-much-wind of peridotite / / Windows ajar for void to pool in / / Resuscitated memory in the cloud clack / / The hurricane's waterlogged house / / Sanguinary / / Stalagmites

/ / Enter lab report of cobalt lethal animal

/ / Enter desolation

/ / Enter stampede on fire escape

/ / Enter tick-tock telluric wind

/ / Enter forensic farmland of crumbled beehive

/ / Enter night cocoon for the perplexed

/ / Enter fallopian tears

/ / Enter showered corneas in each raindrop

/ / Enter scribbled sand built-in on child's hand

II.

The world's globulose reams...

I watched the day beyond
a window of spurs
and green tentacles
] inside the elision where my head rests   you

To be discolored like a slumbering hyphen at the corner of thought

entrenched,

Fording litmus waters with basalt between toes
/\

I struggle to open my fumigating
eye
brine of oyster

becoming
remote as passage
flit through
my innards into unwitnessed light
recoil
in the abscess of interior
having overcome
the feeling of motherhood
best described as wave with walrus tusks

Pomaceous / night detaches petrichor from the coveted earth
involution or delirancy in animal maternal

mind
flits down
spine

resisting the seated ghost of nectar
that sleeping oyster chant bolus of spring,

fording th[is] granular life

Remote deliquescency from where
I emerge uncontained in boundary of water
juiced as rhythm so
vastly unattainable
mute within shadow of thought
ancient craquelure of a winding rock
or bitumen
the
wind
consumes

Discolored in halted meter /\
Algae crystalline
Gale returns to shore
The nether world of not

moss, rock
beats on
rock /
pause in
breath pause(
as) sing-
ing (breath)
chanting
murmur
of rock
in my
ruby
fist of
vestment
& truce

billow
coiling
mother

ocean trellises of hope
ocean murmuring ear

The world's...globulose reams
whose indecency

abjectly overcoming the feeling of motherhood

best described as
internal wind, sweeping carbuncle

weighing
with ash weight
with ash scent
with falling slag

I become deprived porthole
The rock, the rock, the rock
cracked vibrancy
passage into delirant, her parched tongue

Whose sentence slumbers in a box

of remedies
dogma of dilapidated comma fails to
crease the transition between thoughts
The place to which you remain fastened
afterthought cooked by wind
returns vampiric over foliage responding to the sonar
sound of creaking wood
from which I gaze with eyes in trees
scrawled dacite
mouth moving in mourning
of all contemporary rivers

I wait
& I am
a longbow

That gloved my unwitnessed interior
of petrol
an abscess of colors blurred, confounded into one
tender blackness
obsidian gently toeing wind

Eye riveted in oyster glow
        shut by unclaimable seal
        dimeter of trochaics   / /
        rock-rock

        (oh) rock, (oh) rock

        specter dressed in milk
                visible
                        medusa head

I have oppressed you inside my sentence

Now I release you into the air

As wave
or pyre

Oyster silks
glittering eye
deceivingly
at heels of tuff

I become situated in the imperturbable
tunnel opening onto sea

The wind rumbles operatic
Rage, coliseum of hurt

Another sentence slips
amid tones of grey
into a stranger's open
mouth interloper trapped
by straying fly
trickling fangs

because the world is lost
I have a child who waits

While rock remains rock   the wind jostles it

waving walrus tusks
my unwitnessed interior
of tar
the rock
the rock
which speaks
laminating world's body
a rock which
is not steel
a rock which
is not death
a rock which
expels
gases
a rock as
version of
gas
which
is feeble
which is
alive with
life
with
rock
such a rock that listens
to my feeling

to my being
a mother
who waits
in a world
adrift with
inexperienced miracles

(oh) rock, (oh) rock

A cage of coal is maternal crust
   gazing from without without within
molecule mastering tongue
thrashing wind brittle winter

thee eyeless face
   of motherhood sweeps
lowly recompositing each stick
on splashing mud
the ye, thee
staring ribboned light

of t-a-tter
                                        tatter
                                             rettat
                                        tarett
                                                  t
                                                    t
                                                         rock,
                                                         oh singing rock

(In Tempo)

tatter
        rettat
tarett
               t
                  t
tatter
        rettat
tarett
               t
                  t
tatter
        rettat
tarett
               t
                  t

Th(ee) whose scoria melts in outline of ear   wind slips and slurs as
shap(e)d cave.   period, dot, unakite (in the cityscape
of blind ecology

having understood the feeling of motherhood

in the flank of boned light
in the first flank of daylight
souping morning
of hurt
climbing foggily

thee blind ecology fills # rock

as frofre / bracken by / the tip of rock   whose corners coexist /
invisible transmuting / wind into sediment

the eye in simmer of mineral, bleeds

gale in frofre / or blank corset boundary in rock   like motherhood / it does not hush /

a rock
began
scornful
inside
a rock
frofre
oh fro-
fre far
more still
than this
rock, oh
cradle
of dark
water

for Grendel's Mother (1)

ides áglaécwíf
troll's wife, also mother

from lands afar
feorwegum

her neck turns toward grief the gong snakes through gravity
pausing on weight
haunch of áglaécwíf slithering in my groin snapping right-left foot
reticulation

every day I enter the room which is a child's life
the child rubs her eyes, áglaécwíf, mother
whose trollness tastes of figs & diaspora

Ye, her(e)
When I arrive, while she stands more remote than tree

From waters you sprung on my hind / / Boreal third eye
Shrub swamp of icy wetness / / Awaiting brackish flood
Ye undulant grafted corpse / / undergarment of myself

for Grendel's Mother (2)

A scarlet light in my blind ecology
A red blind of ecology
In my tapering blindness
Having licked the feeling of motherhood into paw
Having descended into left breast
Having the scalp on right
Ringworm of solitude
Being inside mother in filmy
Of blind ecology
From blood to toe
Of bodiless
With grey of wending sunrise
On the blossom, of daughter's web

I put on your bloated face
Slurp salt, rub belly
Turn toward time (as it begins)

A fluvial entity
Flesh full of letters
Body collects so much
(The trees)
Begin to stretch

Slide down storm of chestnut hair / /

My ear lays against pumice
Returns with wind
Inside caved containment
Of human ear
What gyres
And listens
As wíggryre wífes or
War-violence of woman

Each ear blushes with sediment
Having become silvery moisture
As calcium floret on ankle:
sprout of bone

When flora speaks
My [wail] distends into stillness
Films, dreadfully pillar
Retinue

Look, my face of motherhood ages
With child's spittle
My face of motherhood prunes the air
Expresses
The rifting clouds

Speak, look, ruminant
Burnt fingertip
That warlike form of losing boundary
That warlike entrail of motherhood

Having understood
Stillness of bush/rock

And sunrise

In pluvial crack the child's finger
        follows a timed expansion of drop

being skilled elision
as forest knows itself

as forest conceals troll's grief
in humus
sorhfulne,

warm as time

supplanted & displaced
ignominy of mecca-child

more than a shatter in fragment of
  broken rhyolite
aching arm reaches as haunch
of flint, the double invisible layer
looking on deep insentience
  rock rubs against this blank language
of morning
surging beneath cloud

evacuation of color drips from
planted face contemplating lily blossom
on this most dirty of ponds
sunk as sorhfulne
as sorh-
full-ness
of rock, (oh) trem-
bling rock

raw / figures in dirt
befalling mother
in after-alien stink of birth
hair, the colonizing stink
of hormonal drippage

in grip of sweat, knowing the nether not, sorhfulne fog on thigh

in vines pooling night
in stillness of web
securely vastness
the smallest shed of animal

I blink by the wet moss
terminally evaporating

Her purple skin cloak (which) covered grief

wif unhyre woman monstrous

Is your belly abending?
Is the stem a-deepening croak?
Much that you do not recognize
alien
in the nether not   having understood the stalked monstrosity of
m(other)
                    having been monstrously covered in vernal grass
  razed & crushed into flat-hooded stillness of foot, a deep mandible

amorphic voiced animal,
woman monstrous
melding
mind to wind
for a nest of granite (oh) pliable

moveable color spectrum
When grass fills rock
grass stammers for
rock-grieving fragment
Wind channels grass-rockiness

Oh rock
devoid
(having been)

As wif unhyre desert incarnate

The flow of water in channel of birth
Bespeaks & preempts unavoidable lash
Mother encomium silk / grass distended

Solitary in a field of blossoms,
I passing through transient landscapes blindly as tree

A sedentary soar

Inside
candes
-cent
stillness
mother
-body
indis
-tinguis
-hable
from ris
-ing schist

"and predating cool fiery"

Understanding the mingling of blood
Time to split light
And in bathing unskin oneself
Of gyre

Gelding daughter scaled as sun becomes
Channel, voiced lung

Mother fissure

For futurity is functional organ
Jest bursting
Forth

You whistled onto the hole (as if summoning its dark insight to dissolve)

In the gestating hole of swirling dampness
A marble stone sleeps

Whistle succumbing

Acutely limber by proxy and defrocked
In naked pond-whistle trembling
To which coal responds

With a hiss

A daughter does not slumber inside her mother
Warlike in trollwidow's light
Progressing from primate mother hoot
Against the freight of consciousness
Incendiary within the rock
That waits in flame
Of deep earth
For a thought
Rusting within
So much fog darkening daylight, novel night
Stillness of gaping mouth
Slumbering in recognizable mother spasm
Indented vestment that turns skin
Appropriated stream of organism
War-violence of wind
From which sprouted silver motherhood
Emerges from slate
Being sonorous bandwidth unfelt by ear

Hemmed within sentence
An imploding if

Boulder whisper fiber
Stained glimmers of a freckled morning

Reflecting on leaf as pond
On quartzite stomach

The upper level of shine in jutting fragment
Whose underside is worm shadow, root nest

Whose overside ribs with carved veins
Of morning dew juice

The sea stack has its grassy hair
The ocean boils beneath

I in space against space
Mass of rudiment quiet, ruby spore

In redness sleep with my poked cheek
Elking rock

Switch into incontestable bitumen
Of neck

The wind nicks at it
Polishing sybil,

Whose masked sibilance I conniving labor
On left breast

To lug
Within wif unhyre

The wind is an experimental ruin
Sculpted grammar of destruction
Engraved as I deck myself in marsh
I don stump now shaped like poetics
Hammering apocalypse to my left deaf ear
A trickle of gesture

Storm upon storm avenging the animal
Murdering the limb, redressing redemption
I with motherhood gathering pebbles in the stony waft of time,
sipping through gelds
Opening,

Closing in this grid
Where parsimonious weather drips at open head
Staring slate collocates feral witness
No longer responsive
A ratty sentience released like spores

Counting stonelets
Every day a rock awakens to new gradation

NOTES:

The following old English is from *Beowulf*:

"frofre" - comfort
"ides áglaécwíf" - troll's wife
"feorwegum" - from far off lands
"wíggryre wífes" - the war-violence of woman
"sorhfulne" - sorrow, woe
"wif unhyre" - monstrous woman

40 fingers
hauling
her pillar
to Heorot

I enter your waters bearing a red skull

Inverted cone
is iron-forged taxonomy

The tarn swells

While sea-monsters weep the blade-melting ice

Wolf, know
Excavated fiendish head

Ingesting swords at the bottom borne weight of dead men. An
alternate: Beowulf's teeth gape on shore, gushing gums color the
water & Grendel's mother's sneer of lightning sears treetops

I sit unfelt by shadow shallowing river broth

Index of first lines

Acknowledgements

Thanks to Jen Tynes of *The Magnificent Field* for publishing an excerpt of this poem in chapbook form. Thanks also to Mary Newell, Bernard Quetchenbach, and Sarah Nolan for including a selection in a special issue of *Dispatches from the Poetry Wars* entitled, "Poetics for the More-Than-Human World," and to rob mclennan of Above/Ground press for printing another excerpt in *Touch the Donkey*.

Love and gratitude to my partner Kristofer J. Petersen-Overton, without whom this poem could not exist. Your comments on multiple versions of How to Make Words of Rubble were invaluable.

To my friend Jessica Baer, thank you for supporting my writing and to Anselm Berrigan for all the advice and mentorship.

Chris Carson and Payton O'Neal of Blue Figure Press, thank you for believing in this manuscript and for your dedication and enthusiasm.

Isabel Sobral Campos is the author of the poetry collection *Your Person Doesn't Belong to You* (Vegetarian Alcoholic Press, 2018), and the chapbooks *Material* (No, Dear and Small Anchor Press, 2015), *You Will Be Made of Stone* (dancing girl press, 2018), and *Autobiographical Ecology* (Above/Ground Press, 2019). Her poetry has appeared in the *Boston Review, Brooklyn Rail*, as well as in the anthologies *BAX 2018: Best American Experimental Writing and Dispatches from the Poetry Wars: Poetics for the More-Than-Human World*. She is the co-founder of the Sputnik & Fizzle publishing series.